Kazan, Russia
Travel and Tourism, Guide

Author
Caleb Gray.

SONITTEC PUBLISHING. All rights reserved. No part of this publication may be reproduced, distributed, or transmitted in any form or by any means, including photocopying, recording, or other electronic or mechanical methods, without the prior written permission of the publisher, except in the case of brief quotations embodied in critical reviews and certain other noncommercial uses permitted by copyright law. For permission requests, write to the publisher, addressed "Attention: Permissions Coordinator," at the address below.

Copyright © 2019 Sonittec Publishing
All Rights Reserved

First Printed: 2019.

Publisher:
SONITTEC LTD
College House, 2nd Floor
17 King Edwards Road,
Ruislip
London
HA4 7AE

Table of Content

- SUMMARY 1
- INTRODUCTION 6
- ABOUT KAZAN... 9
- HISTORY OF KAZAN 18
  - 11TH CENTURY.. 18
    - Foundation of Kazan... 18
  - 13TH CENTURY.. 20
    - Conquest of Volga Bulgaria by the Mongols 20
  - 14TH CENTURY.. 21
    - First mention of Kazan.. 21
  - 15TH CENTURY.. 21
    - Foundation of the Kazan Khanate 21
  - KAZAN KHANATE'S WARS WITH IVAN III 22
  - 16TH CENTURY.. 24
    - Kazan Khanate's Wars with Vasili III 24
    - Kazan Khanate's Wars with Ivan IV the Terrible............. 27
    - Russian Conquest of Kazan.. 28
    - Kazan Kremlin... 30
  - 17TH CENTURY.. 31
    - Development 31
  - 18TH CENTURY.. 32
    - Kazan Governorate and Pugachev Rebellion 32
  - 19TH CENTURY.. 33
    - Kazan Imperial University.. 33
  - 20TH CENTURY.. 34
    - Soviet Period 34
    - After the Soviet Union... 35
  - 21ST CENTURY 35
- TOURISM 37
  - KAZAN QUICK GUIDE 37
    - Getting in.. 37
    - Getting around 40
    - Seeing 42

Doing 51
　　Buy 54
　　Eat 56
　　Sleep 59
　　Stay safe 64
　　Contact 64
　　Getting out 65
DETAILED GUIDE TO KAZAN 73
CUISINE & RESTAURANTS 79
CULTURE: SIGHTS TO VISIT 86
ATTRACTIONS & NIGHTLIFE 91
TIPS FOR TOURISTS 94
PLACES IN KAZAN 97
　　Temple of All Religions 100
　　Qolşärif Mosque 102
　　Soviet Lifestyle Museum 105
　　Suyumbike Tower 107
　　Raifa Monastery 110
　　Museum of 1000 years of Kazan 111
　　House of Zinaida Ushkova 112
　　Peter and Paul Cathedral 113
　　Blagoveshchensky Cathedral 114
　　Bolgar State Historical and Architectural Reserve 115
　　Old Tatar Village 116
BEST THINGS TO DO IN KAZAN, RUSSIA 116
WHAT TO DO IN KAZAN FOR FAMILIES WITH CHILDREN 121

Kazan, Russia

Summary

The importance of travelling in our life?
Everyone has their very own reasons to travel. Some people travel for work, some travel for pleasure while for others it is just a way of life. They travel to live and to escape at the same time.

Whatever might be the reason to travel, here are few ways in which travelling would definitely change you and I think that is why travelling becomes so important in life:

Enjoy being alone: There is something therapeutic about being alone and being at peace with it.

While you soak in a new culture, you also connect with your own inner self.

<u>Learn to adapt</u>**:** It is a different world out there, literally. Be it the pace of life, the language or simply the change in weather, it is always a change and you have to adapt to it. This is what makes travelling truly beautiful as you break away from the routine and adapt to something totally new.

<u>Experience a new culture</u>: Every place comes with its distinct cultural habits, you cannot think about New York without talking about its fast paced life and about Italy without enjoying its relaxed lifestyle. Similarly, while visiting the UK you might have to be a bit formal in your interactions with the locals, on the other hand, while greeting the people in Thailand, one can be really warm and casual.

Broaden your taste buds: Travelling without experiencing the local food is just not complete. It is not only a culinary experience but a cultural one as well.

Get out of comfort zone: From simple experiences like the weather, way of life or food to the more adventurous ones like trying a new sport, travelling really pushes ones boundaries to the core. You might end up participating in a street carnival in Brazil just like the locals or trying the local delicacies (read insects) in Thailand.

Indulge in Photography: It does not matter whether you are a professional or not. It is also irrelevant whether you have a DSLR or a very basic camera, while travelling what matters is the love and quest for seeing beautiful places and the sheer joy of capturing them in your lense. Travelling would in return give you your very own collection of amazing postcards of beautiful sunsets, snow laced mountains or sunny beaches.

<u>Learn to escape</u>: Travelling is the best way to break the routine. If you are in a bustling city, go ahead and experience the country life. If you are in a rural place, travel to a bustling city and experience its madness. Stressed with the city life or work pressure? A spa break in Himalayas or Kerala is a must try.

<u>Appreciate Nature</u>: The quest to explore more when one is travelling always leads to a sense of amazement about nature. While most of us keep a track of technological advancements, Nature has its own ways of outshining all of these. The Antelope Canyon in Arizona or Turquoise Ice in Russia are the finest examples of this. For more, check out the most unbelievable places around the world.

<u>Get closer to your own roots</u>: While one travels and experiences a lot of different cultures and practices, it definitely brings one closer to his or her own roots. Travel helps one appreciate one's identity and culture.

Travelling is all about experiences. They can happen in terms of culture, people, places but most importantly with one's own self and this was all about

Introduction

With a population of about 1.3 million (2011 census), a rich history, deep culture and strong economic influence, thus taking the title from Nizhny Novgorod. By many measures, Kazan has one of the highest standards of living in Russia, following after Moscow and St. Petersburg.

Kazan has just recently earned the reputation of a sports city, due to its recent investments in this domain. Kazan organized the World Summer Universiade 2013, was a host city for FINA World Aquatics Sports Championship in 2015 and the Confederations Cup of 2017, and is also one for the FIFA World Cup in 2018 in Russia. It is said that one of the World Cup semi-finals may be held in Kazan! Both the World Cup and Universiade events are enhancing the city's booming construction. In the last couple of years, sport venues have popped up in Tatar capital, together with residential buildings and offices. Many of Kazan's professional teams, such as Rubin (football) or Ak Bars (hockey), have been recent Russia champions.

Kazan has long been a focal point of higher education in Russia. It remains a university city, with some of Russia's top universities including Kazan Federal University (KFU formerly Kazan State University, TGGPU and the Kazan Finance Institute), Kazan State Technological University (KGTU), Kazan State Technical University (KAI), and KazanState Power Engineering University. Many foreign students study in Kazan, adding diversity to the city's tolerant. Schools in Kazan, and Tatarstan itself, tend to be ones of the best in Russia.

Located between Europe and Asia, having both Russian and Tatar populations, Kazan peacefully blends Muslim and Christian cultures. There are also many other religions represented in Kazan. For example, in the city center there are synagogue and new catholic church. This vibrant city with over 1000 years of history is an excellent travel destination, and the number of tourists visiting is rapidly increasing every year.

About Kazan

As the capital city of the Republic of Tatarstan, Kazan is a glorious city that represents Russia's Tsarist past. With complex palaces, towering churches, and a thriving cultural scene, Kazan is a pure Russian city with incredible beauty and heart.

As the "Third Capital of Russia," there is plenty to see and to do while staying in Kazan. Visitors can enjoy long walks down the streets of the city, as each of them offers a new arrangement of colors and historic buildings. Kazan is also one of the largest economic, political, scientific and cultural centers of the country.

One of the main attractions is the Kazan Kremlin. Built by Ivan the Terrible on the ruins of the palace of the Kazan Khanate that he destroyed, this white fortress is a beautiful sight in any season. The Kremlin of Kazan reflects not only the ethnic mix of Tatars and Russians that make up this important region of the Russian Federation, but also the combined strength of the region's two great religions: Islam and Orthodox Christianity.

The magnificent Kul Sharif Mosque, named for Kazan's last great Imam before Ivan the Terrible invaded and seized the city, is the Kremlin's main jewel. It is the largest Muslim place of worship in Europe, and serves as home to a rich collection of ancient books. As an equally important place of Orthodox worship, the Annunciation Cathedral within Kazan's Kremlin is an architectural gem completed in 1561, 9 years after the city was conquered. The cathedral is said to have been designed by Postnik Yakovlev, the same architect who was said to be blinded after completing St. Basil's Cathedral on Moscow's Red Square.

Today's Kazan appears to be equally strongly tied with its unique mixture of religious beliefs. Philanthropist Ildar Khanov began work on his Temple of All Religions in 1992 near the shores of the Volga River, and this unique building is still under construction. The Temple makes use of religious architecture from all over the world, and has an Orthodox church dome, a minaret, synagogue-like fixtures, and other items representing 16 of the world's many faiths.

In 2005 Kazan celebrated its millennium jubilee. Despite of such venerable age, the city is growing and dynamically developing in all respects. There are lots of museums, libraries, concert halls and theaters. There is even "Ermitazh-Kazan" Center the only branch of the famous museum in Saint Petersburg.

A prevailing feature of life in the city is peaceful, creative coexistence of different religions and nationalities. Due to its gorgeous architecture, breathtaking scenery, and welcoming locals, Kazan is the perfect destination for travelers of all ages.

Kazan places of interest
Kazan has a lot of <u>museums</u>, including 34 state museums, several public and private galleries.

The largest museum of the city is the National Museum of Tatarstan Republic, founded in 1894. You can find the most valuable natural science, archaeological, ethnographic and other exhibitions in the main building of the museum built in 1800-1815 (Kremlin Street, 2).

Inside the Kazan Kremlin, there is a branch of the State Hermitage. Also, the Museum of Fine Arts of the Republic of Tatarstan (Karl Marx Street, 64) and The Museum of Kazan Millennium (Sultan Galiev Square, Pushkin Street, 86) are among the most popular museums in the city.

The city has a large number of theaters. The most famous and popular theaters are:

- ✓ Tatar Academic State Opera and Ballet Theater named after Musa Jalil a venue for international theater and music festivals (Svobody Square, 2),
- ✓ Tatar Academic Theater named after Galiaskar Kamal (Tatarstan Street, 1),
- ✓ Kazan State Academic Russian Bolshoi Drama Theater named after V.I. Kachalov (Bauman Street, 48).

Also, Kazan has a circus (one of the leading in Russia with a unique building) and 12 movie theaters with 61 screens, including Simex 4D.

Concerts, performances and other cultural and entertainment events are held at the State Concert Hall named after S. Saidashev, the cultural-entertaining complex "Pyramid", sports and mixed-use complexes Basket-Hall, Tatneft Arena, the Sports Palace, UNICS and other venues.

Kazan has a lot of parks. The most ones are the amusement park "Kyrlay", Millennium Park, Victory Park, Uritsky Park, Central Park, as well as Russia's oldest and one of the the oldest in Europe, Kazan zoological and botanic garden.

The Kremlin is a favorite destination of tourists coming to Kazan. You can buy a lot of different souvenirs and gifts there.

The historic center of Kazan was rebuilt in 1990-2000s in preparation for the celebration of the millennium of the city. Some historic buildings and monuments were demolished. Today, the most valuable areas in terms of historic buildings are Bauman Street, Kremlin Street, Mushtari Street, Karl Marx Street, Maxim Gorky Street, Gabdulla Tukai Street, Bulak channel area, Svobody Square, Old-Tatar sloboda.

Tourists and pilgrims also visit Peter and Paul Cathedral, Kazan Virgin Monastery, unique historical and architectural complexes of Raif monastery and island-town Sviyazhsk located near Kazan.

In the 21st century, Kazan received several new high-rise buildings. Since 2008, the tallest building in Kazan was the 85-meter 26-storey hotel "Riviera". Today, the tallest skyscraper in Kazan is the 35-storey residential complex "Lazurniye Nebesa" (122 meters).

Kazan transport system

The international airport "Kazan" is located about 26 km to the south-east of the city. A number of domestic (to Moscow, St. Petersburg, Chelyabinsk, Ufa, Ekaterinburg, Novosibirsk, Sochi, and others) and foreign flights (to Almaty, Baku, Dubai, Helsinki, Istanbul and others) are available. The airport was reconstructed in preparation for Kazan 2013 Summer Universiade.

The railway station is located in the central part of Kazan. The main building of the station was constructed in 1896.

Kazan is connected by bus transportation with all the towns of Tatarstan Republic, and neighboring regions. Buses to Naberezhnye Chelny, Chistopol, Nizhnekamsk, Bugulma, Almetyevsk, Bavly, Ufa, Sterlitamak, Ulyanovsk, Samara, Orenburg, Cheboksary, Yoshkar-Ola, Busuluk run from Kazan every day. There are also international routes Kazan Baku, Kazan Aktobe.

History of Kazan
11th Century
Foundation of Kazan

The official date of Kazan's foundation is 1005 and the city held millennium celebrations in 2005. However this official date has been disputed by historians. Some evidence for supposing that Kazan was founded in the 11th century are coins dating from the reign of Duke Wenceslaus I of Bohemia (who reigned from 921 to 935) and other ancient artefacts found in archaeological digs on the territory of the Kazan Kremlin. If Kazan does date from the 11th century it might have been as a trading town on route from Scandinavia to the

Middle East and part of Volga Bulgaria, whose capital was Bolgar which is located 130km from Kazan.

The origins of the name Kazan are also debated, but the most common belief is that it is after the Turkic word for a heavy cooking pot and there is an often repeated legend in relation to this. According to this legend a son of a Volga Bulgarian khan stopped in what became Kazan and ordered his servant to get some water using his golden kazan, but upon doing so the servant slipped and dropped the kazan in the river. Afterwards the river became known as the Kazanka and the city which developed next to the river became known as Kazan.

A further legend surrounding early Kazan is the legend of Zilant the giant winged snake-like dragon. The legend states that when the first settlers arrived the land where Kazan now stands was infested with snakes who were led by Zilant, which is the Tatar word for snake. To rid the land of snakes a sorcerer recommended putting down lots of dry branches. In the winter all the snakes nested in the branches which the settlers then set alight. The snakes were burned alive and any which escaped were slain. Finally Zilant himself appeared and the bravest of the Tatar knights cut him into six pieces. Now statues of Zilant appear around the city as well as on the city's flag and coat of arms.

13th Century

Conquest of Volga Bulgaria by the Mongols

In 1236 the Mongols conquered Volga Bulgaria, devastated its centres Bolgar and Bilyar and broke it up into several vassal states of the Golden Horde. As a result Kazan, which was possibly previously a Volga Bulgar settlement, grew in importance as refugees from Bolgar and Bilyar resettled there.

14th Century
First mention of Kazan
The first written evidence of the existence of Kazan came in 1391 in the Rogozhsky Chronicle where it was mentioned as being the centre of a Bolgar sultanate.

15th Century
Foundation of the Kazan Khanate
In either 1437 or 1438 Kazan was conquered by Oluğ Möxämmäd the deposed khan of the Golden Horde, who founded the Kazan Khanate with Kazan as its capital. From his new khanate Oluğ was able to launch raids on the Moscow Principality and from 1439 onwards his raids penetrated deep into Russian lands. In spring 1445

Grand Prince Vasili II of Moscow was even captured by the Kazan Tatars and the Russians were forced to pay a large ransom for their grand prince and sign a treaty beneficial for the Kazan Khanate. Oluğ died in 1145 shortly after his return to Kazan and was succeeded by his son Mäxmüd. Mäxmüd was subsequently succeeded by his sons, firstly Xälil in approximately 1465 and then Ibrahim in 1467.

Kazan Khanate's Wars with Ivan III

Russia's new leader, Grand Prince Ivan III, wished to help his ally Khan Qasim of Kasimov (a son of Oluğ Möxämmäd) win the Kazan throne which he considered his by right and the Russo-Kazan War of 1467-1469 began. In September 1469 after many setbacks Russian troops were able to besiege Kazan and cut its access to water, forcing them to sue for peace. A peace treaty beneficial to the Russians was signed resulting in the release of many Russian prisoners.

Khan Ibrahim died in 1479 and, after a power struggle, was succeeded by his son Ilham. Khan Ilham's brother Möxämmät Ämin, like Qasim before him, decided to flee Kazan and went to Moscow to serve Grand Prince Ivan III. In 1484 Ilham was disposed by the pro-Moscow faction in Kazan and the young Möxämmät Ämin was made khan. However Möxämmät Ämin was not to reign for long as he in turn was disposed the next year and Ilham returned. Angered by losing his candidate in Kazan, in 1487 Ivan III launched another campaign again Kazan and managed to capture Ilham and once again install Möxämmät Ämin on the throne. From this time Ivan III started to use the title duke of Bulgaria as well as his other titles.

Möxämmät Ämin was always under the influence of Moscow and in 1495 a faction decided to replace him with Mamuq. However Mamuq soon proved to be unpopular and he was forced to flee. Rather than having Möxämmät Ämin back, Kazan nobles asked Ivan III to send them Möxämmät Ämin's brother Ğäbdellatíf. However he soon also became unpopular and the nobles once again asked Ivan III to re-establish Möxämmät Ämin as khan.

16th Century

Kazan Khanate's Wars with Vasili III

In 1505 in anticipation of the death of Ivan III and spurred on by his wife, Möxämmät Ämin decided to assert his independence from Moscow. He massacred many Russians within the Kazan Khanate and invaded Russia. Russia was taken completely by surprise by these actions of her once loyal ally. After Ivan III's death, Grand Prince Vasili III sent troops against Kazan to assert his authority over the khanate. Despite a crushing victory over the Russians at the Battle of Arsk Field in 1506, Möxämmät Ämin nevertheless decided to sue for peace and paid homage to Vasili III. Khan Möxämmät Ämin died in 1518 without an heir.

After Möxämmät Ämin's death the 11-year old Khan Şahğäli of Kasimov was invited to be khan of Kazan. Şahğäli was completely controlled by Moscow making him unpopular in Kazan which led to him being deposed by nobles in 1521 who had entered into a conspiracy with Sahib Geray, brother of Khan Mehmed I Geray of Crimea, who was hostile to Russia. Russians within the Kazan Khanate were once again massacred. Later in 1521 combined Kazan and Crimean Tatar forced led a devastating raid on Russia which ended in a siege of Moscow and Vasili III paying a tribute to Crimea.

In 1524 when Russia sent a massive army against Kazan led by Prince Ivan Belsky. Belsky started to besiege Kazan but when the city sued for peace, Belsky had no choice to accept as he did not have enough supplies to continue, an act with was deemed treasonous in Moscow. Khan Sahib Geray though was more interested in Crimean affairs and decided to return there, leaving the Kazan Khanate to his 14 year old nephew Safa Geray.

Vasili III's final war with Kazan came in spring 1530 after the Russian ambassador to Kazan was offended and a new war broke out between Russian and Kazan. Even though Kazan was able to reinforce its defences during the previous period of peace, the Russians troops managed to break through the outer defences and started to besiege the city causing Khan Safa Geray to flee. Russian commanders missed their chance to seize a deserted city before Kazan troops returned and launched a damaging strike on the Russians forcing them to eventually abandon the siege. The two sides entered peace talks. A conspiracy had previously been formed against Khan Safa Geray and a group of Kazan nobles requested that Canğäli (brother of Khan Şahğäli) be nominated as their new Khan. Canğäli arrived in Kazan in 1530/1531 and ruled the khanate under the domination of his Moscow protectors.

Kazan Khanate's Wars with Ivan IV the Terrible

Khan Canğäli only reigned until 1535 when he was ousted in a conspiracy of Kazan nobles who returned the throne to Safa Geray. Canğäli was murdered during the struggle, and not only did Safa Geray take his throne but also his widow Söyembikä. Russia, now ruled by a young Ivan IV (Ivan the Terrible), had to once again deal with the Tatar threat from Crimea and Kazan. Russian preparations for an invasion of Kazan had to be cancelled in 1541 to defend the country against a Crimean invasion.

Khan Cangäli only reigned until 1535 when he was ousted in a conspiracy of Kazan nobles who returned the throne to Safa Geray. Cangäli was murdered during the struggle, and not only did Safa Geray take his throne but also his widow Söyembikä. Russia, now ruled by a young Ivan IV (Ivan the Terrible), had to once again deal with the Tatar threat from Crimea and Kazan. Russian preparations for an invasion of Kazan had to be cancelled in 1541 to defend the country against a Crimean invasion.

Russian Conquest of Kazan

Russia's crucial battle came in 1552 as Ivan the Terrible prepared for a full scale invasion of Kazan. Russian troops were based at the Sviyazhsk

Fortress which was established nearby the previous year after having been constructed in Uglich and sailed down the Volga. Ivan commanded an army of 150,000 which started to besiege Kazan in August 1552. Prince Aleksandr Gorbaty-Shuisky was able to defeat the Tatar cavalry units around Arsk and Prince Andrey Kurbsky destroyed the Mari army. In addition military engineers managed to cut off Kazan's water supply. The city was almost ready to fall.

A siege tower was constructed but it would have been destroyed by Kazan's artillery. It was the engineer named Rozmysl (it is believed this was actually a name given to an English expert), who dealt the final blow. Rozmysl was able to blow up the walls of the fortress allowing Russian troops to pour into the city and slaughter all those who couldn't escape in time. Khan Yädegär Möxämmäd was captured and sent back to Moscow and religious leader Qol-Şärif was killed. After decades of war between Moscow and Kazan, Tsar Ivan the terrible had finally conquered the city. Guerrilla warfare continued for several years afterwards but this too was finally crushed by 1556.

Kazan Kremlin

Immediately following the Conquest of Kazan, Tsar Ivan the Terrible ordered that a stone kremlin be built on the location of Kazan's old fortress. Pskov expert architects were brought in to construct the 1,800 metres of walls and 13 towers. Ivan also proceeded with bringing in Russian settlers as well as russifying the surviving Tatars and converting them to Orthodoxy. Loyal Tatars were allowed to settle outside of the centre in what developed into the Staraya Tatarskaya Sloboda. In 1555 the Kazan Eparchy was established and it was decided to replace a wooden church which had been hastily constructed in the kremlin after the conquest with a stone cathedral. It was completed in 1562 with the work being overseen by Postnik Yakovlev, who previously worked on St Basil's Cathedral in Moscow which was built to commemorate the victory over Kazan.

17th Century
Development
Throughout the 17th century, Kazan developed, now as part of Russia, both economically and in terms of population, becoming a regional centre for manufacturing. Adam Olearius, the ambassador of Holstein-Gottorp visited Kazan in 1634 and described the city as being surrounded by an outer wooden fortress with a stone kremlin in the centre. He went on to say how both Russians and Tatars inhabited the city but the Tatars were forbidden to enter the kremlin under pain of death.

18th Century

Kazan Governorate and Pugachev Rebellion

In 1708 Kazan became the administrative centre of the Kazan Governorate. In 1718 Peter the Great issued an edict establishing the Kazan Admiralty which made use of Kazan's timber supplies to build ships for Peter's naval campaigns. Catherine the Great visited Kazan in 1767 and decided to abolish the restrictions on building mosques in the city, facilitating the architectural development of the Staraya Tatarskaya Sloboda. Kazan's development went off track during the rebellion of Yemelyan Pugachev, who managed to capture all of the city apart from the kremlin. Pugachev and his rebels were forced to leave the city after fires broke out. Much of the city was destroyed as a result of the fire. In 1781 Catherine granted Kazan a coat of arms depicting the mythical winged snake Zilant and in 1782 approved a new regulated general plan.

19th Century
Kazan Imperial University

In 1804 the Kazan Imperial University was established by Emperor Alexander I. The university quickly became known as a centre for the sciences, especially in the sphere of organic chemistry. In 1844 Lev Tolstoy started studying law and eastern languages at the university but eventually dropped out. Another famous student of the university who did not finish his course was Vladimir Uyanov (Lenin), who started studying law there in August 1887. Whilst at the university the young Lenin also dedicated a lot of his time to reading the works of Marx and Engels. In December 1887 Lenin was expelled from the university for taking part in a student protest. After his experience in Kazan,

Lenin became even more determined to continue his struggle against the autocracy and the bourgeois.

20th Century
Soviet Period
The Russian Revolution spread to Kazan in 1917. However on the 5 August 1918 the White Army, supported by the Czechoslovak Legion, reached Kazan and, after engaging in battle with the Red Guards based there, the city was captured on 6 August 1918. Located in the city at the time was Russia's gold reserves which had been evacuated to Kazan during the First World War. The Reds were eventually able to recapture the city on 10 September 1918 although most of the Whites were able to escape.

In 1920 Kazan became the capital of the Tatar Autonomous Socialist Soviet Republic within Soviet

Russia. The Second World War saw many factories being evacuated from the west of the Soviet Union to Kazan, making Kazan an industrial centre during the war producing many tanks and planes.

After the Soviet Union

Although there was a separatist movement for an independent Tatarstan or a union of Volga and Ural Islamic nations after the fall of the Soviet Union, in 1992 Kazan instead became the centre of the Republic of Tatarstan, a constituent entity of the Russian Federation.

21st Century

Millennium Celebrations

In 2005 Kazan celebrated its millennium and in the run up to the anniversary the city and its kremlin (which was made a UNESCO World Heritage Site in 2000) was renovated. The Qol-Şärif Mosque was built inside the kremlin and the Kazan Metro became the first one to be opened in Russia after the fall of the Soviet Union. In addition to this the Pope gave his permission to give Russia the Vatican copy of the Our Lady Kazan Icon, one of the most revered copies of the lost original. In 2005 the icon was ceremoniously returned to Kazan where is it now housed in the Kazansky Bogoroditsky Monastery. Since 2009 Kazan has been permitted to call itself Russia's third capital after Moscow and St Petersburg. The city is an important centre for sport and held the 2013 Summer Universiade and will also be a venue during the 2018 Football World Cup.

Tourism
Kazan Quick Guide
Getting in

By plane

Kazan International Airport (IATA: KZN) is 30km to the southeast of the city centre. Aeroflot, S7, Transaero and UTAir fly between Kazan and Moscow, and Rossiya Airlines also flies to Kazan from Saint Petersburg. Finnair, Flydubai, Turkish Airlines and Air Baltic, Azal, Air Astana are some of the international carriers flying to Kazan. International travellers may enjoy shorter queues at passport check compared to overcrowded Moscow airports.

Travelers can take taxi to/from the airport, it takes about 25 minutes. Rates to the downtown start at 450 Rubles, it is recommended to use city taxi that can be ordered by phone call or any taxi app (Uber, Yandex.Taxi, Gett etc.). As of January 2016, foreigners may be asked for 1000 Rubles to city center, although with the taxometer it is 500 (to Bauman Street), so use your negotiation skills. To make you arrival more comfortable, there is Tourist Information Office near domestic flights arrival zone. English-speaking friendly personnel will help you to get a taxi, to book a hotel and provide you all the necessary for your trip information completely for free. There is an Aeroexpress train which can take you to Kazan train station from the airport for 40 RUB in 30 minutes. It only goes every 2 hours even during airport peak hours.

By train

Kazan, Russia

Kazan is easy to reach by train, as it is a major station stop for several west-east trains. Depending on the train, travel from Moscow's Kazan Station can be as short as 11 hours. A direct train from St. Petersburg's Moscow Station takes 25 hours. Kazan's railway station (also known as 'Kazan-1' is located close to the city center, with several hotels, restaurants, and the Kremlin within walking distance of the train station. Note that the ticketing office is not in the main (historic red brick) building, but in the more modern building with a clock tower next door; as one faces the main building from the street, the ticket office is to the left.

The Vosstanie-Passazhirskaya railway station (also known as 'Kazan-2', or 'Vosstanie Pass' on timetables) is located in the northern part of Kazan and connected to Severny Vokzal metro station.

By boat
Kazan has a riverboat terminal on the Volga River and can be reached by river cruise as well. River cruises down the Volga operate during the summer months (early May to end of September). Dozens of boats operated by different companies run from Moscow to Astrakhan. One way or return cruises may be reserved to/from practically any city along the Volga. Turflot.ru and infoflot.ru are several sites that offer tours.

Getting around

Much of the city center is walkable, and the main attractions for tourists (the Kremlin and Bauman Street) are only for pedestrian traffic. Public buses are abundant and cheap, but one must have some knowledge of Russian to read the signs or ask where the buses are headed. Bus system maps are apparently hard to come by. Taxis are available and operate mostly an on-call service, rather than plying the streets for fares. They also congregate at a few taxi stands in predictable places such as the train station. A Metro system is being developed, with eleven stations on the red line in operation as of late 2018, running between Aviastroitelnaya and Dubravnaya.

A free map is distributed at the reception of hotels.

You can rent a bike from one of several Veli'k stands placed in the centre of the city, but as it requires usage of credit card, the registering procedure might be confusing. Here are some of alternative places to rent a bicycle from:

- ✓ Ziferblat (Clockface), Universitetskaya st., 14 (enter from the back of the building, then follow the stairs to the very top).

This is originally a coworking space/cafe, so try to explain their friendly staff that you need one of the bikes to ride. After leaving some kind of ID (standard procedure for sports equipment rental in Russia), you'll be off with one of the cheapest bikes for rent in town (2 roubles/min for the first hour, then the price gets reduced to 1 rouble/min.) +7 843 253 5219

Seeing

Kazan celebrated its 1000-year anniversary in 2005, for which the city got a major facelift. Visitors today will be able to see many of the reconstructed or newly-constructed sites from the anniversary celebration.

Kazan Kremlin
Once a Tatar fortress, it was largely destroyed by Ivan the Terrible. During the 16th and 17th Centuries, Russians reconstructed the Kremlin with new fortifications and Russian institutions (such as the Annunciation Cathedral). Many of the features

of the Kremlin reflect Russian influence of that era, and the construction of the parapets and watchtowers is particularly reminiscent of other dominant Russian cities of the time, such as Pskov and Novgorod. Entry to the Kremlin is through the white clock tower (the Spasskaya Tower) at the end of Bauman Street. Entry costs 300 Rubles with a guided tour, or 20 Rubles to explore the grounds on one's own. There are several interesting things to see inside the Kremlin, including:

✓ Suyumbike Tower

The legend of the Suyumbike Tower is that the Tatar Princess Suyumbike was betrothed to Ivan the Terrible, but she consented to marry him only if he could build the highest tower in Kazan in seven days. Ivan accomplished the task, but Suyumbike, rather than subjugating herself and the Tatar people to the Russian ruler, climbed to the top of the tower and jumped to her death. Locals do not seem to believe that the legend is true, but they appreciate the romanticism of it. At present, the tower is not open to climb the stairs.

✓ Kul-Sharif Mosque

Named after the 16th-century Tatar imam who died defending Kazan from Ivan the Terrible's army, the Kul-Sharif Mosque was completed in 2005 after ten years of construction. It is located within the Kremlin walls, making the Kremlin facility now a symbol of multicultural harmony in multiethnic Tatarstan. Entry to the mosque is free, although visitors must pay 3 Rubles for plastic slip-covers for their shoes in order to keep the floors clean. Visitors who climb the stairs to the third floor observation balcony do not need to remove their shoes. The prayer hall on the ground floor is open only to men going to pray and the second floor balcony is for Muslim women to pray. All women, though, should cover their hair in all parts of the mosque.

From the observation balcony, visitors can appreciate the beauty of the mosque, which is built in a modern design not unlike modern Turkish mosques. The dome in the shape of a lotus flower and the many windows give the prayer hall a bright and airy atmosphere. One uniquely local feature in the mosque is the malachite columns on the minbar (the free-standing pulpit). Some of the 99 names of God are inscribed on the inside of the upper dome and on the window glass, and the name Mohammed is written in a blue disk at the front of the prayer hall. Verses from the Koran, including an incantation against envy, are written on tile in the four corners of the hall, and the names on disks suspended lower in the hall are those of the four rightly-guided caliphs and some of the early prophets.

An interesting Museum of Islam is located below the ground floor of the mosque. Entrance is free, and a tour in English may be available if the English-speaking docent is on duty. The museum also has a booklet in English that explains the exhibits that can be helpful. Some of the exhibits include displays regarding the status of Tatar language in the Soviet era, some history of the building of the mosque (note the photo of prayers being held outdoors in the 1990s before the mosque was built), and on the lower sublevel is a history of Islam in Tatarstan, which mentions of Empress Elizabeth's attempt to convert Tatars to Christianity and Catherine the Great's edict allowing mosques to be constructed.

Kul Sharif Mosque

- ✓ Annunciation Cathedral
- ✓ State Hermitage Museum in Kazan

Affiliated with the Hermitage Museum in St. Petersburg, this museum sometimes has special exhibits of interest.

- ✓ State Museum of the Tatar State and the Republic of Tatarstan

The museum was one of several projects completed for the 1000-year anniversary celebration, and it is located on the former site of the Tatar sultan's mosque, which was destroyed by Ivan's army and a residence (?) was built in its place. The building fell into disrepair over the years and a Turkish company completed the renovations for the 2005 museum opening.

One must first enter on the ground floor (located just to the left of the Suyumbike Tower) and pay the 20-Ruble entry fee. A group of energetic and chatty old ladies staff the museum, although none speak much English. The ground floor section of the museum is filled with gifts to Tatarstan from foreign dignitaries on the occasion of the 1000-year anniversary, as well as a reproduction of the sultan's throne (note the gold dome of the Koran case, which is meant to hold the Koran higher than the sultan's chair) and a reproduction of the mausoleum of the sultans, the original of which is said to be underground nearby: a small square monument marks the spot in the square outside the museum.

To reach the second story of the museum, one must go outside and around the corner and climb the stairs in the courtyard near the Suyumbike Tower. There is no cashier on the second floor, so visitors much go to the ground floor section first. The second floor includes a narrative history of Tatarstan, from the early settlement of the Volga-

Bulgars to the early Tatar state to Tatar Autonomous Soviet Socialist Republic to Tatarstan in the Russian Federation. The guide will insist that visitors also visit a small room on the side where medals and decorations given to the president are displayed.

Bauman Street
The pedestrian zone that stretches between the Kremlin and Tokai Square and the Hotel Tatarstan. This is Kazan's Arbat, with boutiques, souvenir shops and kiosks, cafes, bars, and plenty of opportunities for people-watching. The statuary (such as a bronze carriage) is especially interesting.

Soviet Lifestyle Museum, Ul. Ostrovskaya 39/6 ; Ul. Universitetskaya (*A minute's walk from Ulitsiya Baumana, above, 'Dublin' Irish bar.*). 10-18. By far Kazan's most original and eccentric museum. The museum's curator, Rustem, is an outgoing, friendly, welcoming guy. He is also very knowledgeable about anything related to 'Soviet' culture. Entering the museum is like going through a time-machine back to the USSR. Rustem has managed to acquire anything and everything from the "Soviet" period. He is also bubbling with stories and anecdotes of how "then" compares to "now". Drop by on Sunday afternoons for impromptu Soviet songs jam sessions, complete with guitars, bass, drums, tambourines, bongos, flutes, fog machines and strobe lights. This place is too fun to be named a museum and is interactive in the fullest sense. Well worth the price. A must see if you're in, or anywhere near, Kazan. Cheap.

<u>The Temple of all Religions</u> On the outskirts of Kazan. Take bus number 2 from the center. Interesting building for architecture buffs as it features 16 towers dedicated to different religions. The complex was damaged by fire in April 2017, it is under construction but possible to go inside.

Doing

Kazan offers a lot of various events you can visit during your stay here international opera and ballet festival, different types of music festivals, popular singers concerts and many other interesting things to do. Cirque du Soleil regurlary brings its shows to Kazan. And a must-see event in Tatarstan is a national holiday Sabantuy tatar summer festival, which is celebrated in the beginning of June.

In summer 2013 four double-decker buses began circulating along their routes in Kazan by "City Sightseeing" company. Tourists will ride on them through the city's downtown and see the main attractions, historical landmarks, and architectural beauties of Tatarstan's capital with their own eyes, and not merely see them, but also learn many interesting things about them. The two-level tour buses have been equipped with an audio guide.

The audio recording designed to acquaint guests will the city functions in eight languages: Russian, Tatar, English, French, Spanish, German, Turkish, and Chinese.

List of events to visit:

- ✓ International opera festival named after Fedor Shalyapin annually in February.
- ✓ Russian festival of Folklore "Karavon" annually in May.
- ✓ International festival of classic ballet named after Rudolf Nuriev annually in May.
- ✓ Summer tatar festival Sabantuy annually in June.
- ✓ International handicraft festival "Spasskaya Yarmarka" in Elabuga city annually in August.
- ✓ International jazz music festival "Jazz v usadbe Sandetskogo" annually in August.

- ✓ International open-air opera festival "Kazanskaya osen" (Kazan autumn) annually in September or 30th of August. Entrance is free.
- ✓ Kazan International festival of Muslim cinema annually in September.

Besides events, from the river station (речной вокзал) (close to the bus station, автовокзал) you can take boat trips on the Volga. Two-hour boat trips, without any stops, depart a few times a day (12.00, 15.00 and 19.00 on most days) for 180r. You can also take regular services to different places. To the river station you can take trolleybus 4 or 3 from Koljco (Tukaya sq). There are also various buses from other places; the river station is usually the terminal stop. The walk to the river station from the train station is very nice. Cross the railway tracks at the train station over the eastern bridge and follow the water for 20-30 minutes.

Buy

Souvenirs from Kazan reflects Tatar culture and ethnic colour. You can buy items with national ornaments and scenes from tatar folk tales, mosque figurines and many others.

The most popular souvenir, that each tourist want to buy, is tatar national male headwear "Tubeteika".

Tatar national handicrafts is especially known for its unique leather art and tanning. This kind of very soft, yet long wearing leather called "safyan". Using ancient technologies, craftsmen make amazing items from leather shoes, bags, slippers, keyfob and etc.

Shopping and entertainment centers you can visit are:

- ✓ "Mega" is for a family holiday. It's really all organically combined: a relaxing atmosphere conducive to the implementation of the shopping, places for recreation and leisure, entertainment venues.

- ✓ "Koltso". The name of the shopping center "The Ring" was due to the location. It is an area that many residents of Kazan call the "Ring." It appeared in the city in 1768, and the project is creating the architect Vasily Kaftyrev. Historical background, and a convenient location shopping and entertainment areas account for its huge popularity.

- ✓ "GUM". Updated GUM is a 6 floors, which have clothes, shoes, accessories, jewelry and watch showrooms, shops Perfumery and cosmetics. In restaurants and cafes you can find a wide variety of Russian, Tatar, European, Oriental, Chinese, Mexican and Syrian cuisine.

- ✓ "TSUM". was founded in 1940. The complex is located in the historical center of Kazan, and has a rich past. TSUM always changes with the city, and today it is a large shopping complex with a convenient location and ample car parking.

Eat

Baumana Street has the largest collection of restaurants, cafes, and bars in the city. They range from acceptable to tourist traps. Places to eat off Bauman Street include:

<u>Bilyar</u> An inexpensive restaurant serving Tatar food. The rustic interior is designed to look like the interior of a Tatar log cabin, and a few even have salad bars that look like wells. Main courses are 50-200 Rubles. Try their 'echpekmoks' with bullion, salad 'makhebet', and their Tatar version of 'ukha' or creamy fish soup. At all locations, quality has

been a constant. For desert, try their chak-chak. 4 locations in the city: Ulitsa Butlerova 31 (up the hill behind the Tatarstan Hotel), Ulitsa Vishnevskovo 15 and Prospekt Pobedi 50a (the latter two are a little farther from the center).

Sofra Kebab, Baumana Street 51, 3rd Floor (*In GUM, in the food court on the 3rd floor.*). 10am-10pm. Excellent Turkish cuisine, at a small cafe, located on the 3rd floor of GUM on Baumana Street. This is the very center of Kazan. There are a few Turkish-run places in Kazan's center, but Sofra Kebab provides the best quality/price ratio by a long shot. The prices are very democratic for what you get. Order any main dish and receive a free drink and side dish. Many of the main dishes in Turkish can be found here.

This includes delicacies such as "doner"/shwarma wraps (grilled chicken, wrapped in flat bread with vegetables), Adana Kebab, Beyti Kebab (excellent, w/garlic yogurt sauce), and Kulbasta grilled chicken. The beef or lamb shashlik is also excellent. All will be grilled fresh, right in front of you. They also have great deserts, including marinated walnuts and dates, vanilla rice pudding and of course, some of the best bakhlava to be found in Kazan. If you're in the center and tired of standard Russian or Tatar fare, head over to Sofra Kebab. They also have a good "bizness lunch" special. There are three additional Sofra Kebab locations (Uzhni Shopping Center, near Moskovsky Rynok, etc). Cheaply Priced.

<u>Priyut Kholostyaka</u> A trendy restaurant with an eclectic menu of European and Russian dishes. Main courses 300-500 Rubles. Clean, quiet, and a bit off the tourist path, this is a good place for relaxing and having tea. Although its name means Bachelor's Refuge which makes it sound like a strip

club or something, it is nothing of the sort. Ulitsa Chernishevskovo 27a.

Self-caterers can find a large supermarket (one of the Bakhetle chain) in the TsUM bulding across from the Mirage Hotel. The bakery across from the Milena Hotel on Tazi Gizzata Street has excellent bread and a few groceries.

Хинкальная, Universitetskaya 14, 1st floor. Moscow's famous khinkalnaya comes to Kazan! A great place for Georgian cuisine, with amazing khinkali. Slated to open on September 22, 2013.

Sleep
Budget
I&I Hostel, Bolshaya Krasnaya st, 45, +7(960)044-12-49. Cosy hostel at the centre of a city. English speaking staff. There is a kafe inside, games, music, fun and etc.

<u>Oranjin Hostel</u>, Pushkina 1, 3rd floor (*20 minutes walking from train station*), 8 843 248-01-49, checkin: 12:00; checkout: 12:00. 2.4.6 bedrooms. Guest kitchen, free WiFi, cosy common room. E-mail for booking: Prices start at 500 rub per bed.

<u>Bulgaru Hostel</u>, Universitetskaya street 4/34 ap.8 (*In historical center of Kazan*), (843) 267-18-80. checkin: 11:00; checkout: 11:00. Founded in 2007 as a family enterprise by Ekaterina Bulgaru and Timur Kamalov. Their concept and major ambition is to combine the care and comfort of a family hotel with the fun and free atmosphere of a student's hostel. While offering a 24-hour reception and placing no formal constraints on guests like some old Soviet-era hotels, they don't limit themselves to providing only basic utilities. Wifi is free. 1 bed in day 500 rub.

Aillin Hostel, Bauman street 22 (*Central part of Kazan*), 8 (843) 297-99-71. This is a new hostel, next to the Kremlin, which advertises a friendly atmosphere and cleanliness. From 500 rub/night.

Hostel Kremlin, Bolshaya Krasnaya street 8 (*Central part of Kazan*), 8 (843) 233-07-88. Hostel has conceptual design; it's decorated in the spirit of Kazan attractions. Walking down the hall, you can feel like you are on the one of the main streets Tatarstan capital. . From 600 rub/night.

Midrange
Milena Hotel, Tazi Gizzata Street 19 (*From the train station, make an immediate right, walk one block, and turn* left *at the gas station*), (843) 292-99-92. A new, clean, quiet hotel within walking distance from the train station, and also easy walking distance from Bauman Street and the Kremlin. Note that there is no elevator in the building, so

request a first-floor room if that is important to you. Rooms start at 600 Rubles.

Hotel Shushma, Narimanova Street 19, (843) 292-98-21. Next door to the Milena hotel, and quite comparable to it.

Hotel Volga, 1 Said-Galeeva (*A short walk north of the train station*), (843) 292 14 69. Check if they say that there are no cheap rooms available.clean and basic single rooms from 750 rubles.

Motel Gostinyi Dvorik, Gor'kovskoye shossey St, 47, (843) 260-05-60

Splurge

Courtyard Kazan, 6 Karl Marx Street, Vakhitovskiy District, +7 (843) 567 4000. checkin: 16:00; checkout: 12:00. The rooms have large windows with Kazan Kremlin views. The hotel's Lobby Bar has an innovative setting and relaxed atmosphere and a free WiFi. Full American-style breakfast buffet in main restaurant. Roof Bar with Kazan city views and tasty cocktails. Location near the Kazan Kremlin and main Kazan corporations.

Mirage hotel, (*Directly across from the Kremlin*), (843) 278-05-05. Easily the most expensive hotel in Kazan, but in a prime location with the greatest number of amenities. Rack rate starting at over 6000 rubles.

Shalyapin Palace, (*Bauman Street*), (843) 238-28-00 . Within international standards of service and comfort. Starting at 2600 rubles per person.

Suleiman Palace, Peterburgskaya Street 55, (843) 278-16-16. Comparable in class of service to the Shalyapin Palace, but a bit further away from the city center. The Kremlin is not walkable from here, but it can be reached by a short taxi ride or bus. Rooms start at about 2500 rubles.

Stay safe

Since the '70s, Kazan has long the reputation of being one of the least safe cities of Russia. The "Kazan phenomenon" of street gangs even became a journalistic and sociological concept. However, since the late '90s, the situation has changed fundamentally. Kazan has become a host city for a lot of large international events. As a result there was a modernization of police, so crime rate decreased significantly. For example, during WORLD SUMMER UNIVERSIADE in 2013, a lot of citizens and guests shared their impressions, that they felt safe like never before, even walking in the city centre at night.

Contact

Internet cafes and restaurants with WiFi are found throughout the city. Probably the most useful internet cafe for travelers is a small one across from the train station. From the main station building, cross through the park and cross the main street. It is at the corner to one's left, but hidden behind a newspaper stand and some kiosks.

The post office in Kremlyovskaya St. has seven computers with internet access, for around 36 rub./hour. Pay in advance at the register. Your unspent minutes will be refunded.

Tattelecom on the corner of Baumana and Pushkina, opposite the Koljco mall, has computers with ok Internet for 48 r per hour. Up Pushkina there are a few cafes and restaurants with free unprotected wifi. Also, outside of the Subway restaurant further up on Pushkina there is free unprotected wifi. Mcdonalds also has free wifi (on Baumana and by the train station).

Getting out

<u>The Raifa Monastery</u> In 30 miles from Kazan, on the shore of a beautiful lake, in the middle of the forest, behind a white granite wall, in the center of a great National Park you will find one of the pearls of 17th century Russian architecture: the Raifa Bogoroditsky Monastery. The greatest object of this monastery is the Georgian Mother of God icon, which in its day was venerated as a miraculous object with the power to heal the sick. Today the Raifa Monastery is among the most-visited in the world. The grounds of the monastery are located within the Volga-Kama National Park, where the terrain is a combination of southern taiga and deciduous forests. The park's botanical garden features more than 400 species of exotic plants from North America, Asia and Europe

<u>Ancient city of Bolgar</u> The National Park of Bolgar is one of few historical-architectural complexes left by the Volga Tatars. It is located on the bank of the

Volga 120 km away from Kazan. Bolgar is related with the such names as Pushkin, Peter the Great, Catherine the Great, Kul Gali and many other famous people. It is a sacred place for all Tatars, a place of pilgrimage for Muslims, and a place generally steeped in legend and history.

The National Park of Bolgar is an object of historical and cultural significance. In 1998 the Bolgar Historical-Architectural Complex was included in the provisional list of UNESCO World Heritage sites of the Russian Federation. In National Park of Bolgar you can visit Museum of Bakery, a museum of archaeology (at the time of writing this has yet to fully open), monuments of Islamic architecture from the 13th-14th centuries.

To get there, buses depart from Kazan's South Bus Station (which itself can be reached by taking the number 22 bus from anywhere along Karl Marx

Street in the city centre) at 14:00 and 17:45, while buses return from Bolgar at 05:30 and 13:30. The only hotel, the Hotel Regina, is located at the very north end of the town. Room rates start from 1,300 Rubles. Food options are limited, as expected, but an assortment of cheap eateries and a reasonably well-stocked supermarket can be located near the town's bus station.# Finally, entry to the site is free, although visitors may be charged for entry to the museums.

<u>Island-town Sviyazhsk</u> The place where the Sviyaga River flows into the Volga forms the idea for Push¬kin's lively tale of the Island of Buyan. Sviyazhsk was built by Ivan the Terrible as a fortress for the siege of Kazan, and it went on to become the first Orthodox Christian city in our area, the center of the spread of Christianity. The island also became home to the Uspensky

monastery and the Ioanno-Predtechensky nunnery.

The architectural composition of today's Sviyazhsk includes perfectly preserved churches, such as the antique wooden Troitskaya Church (built in 1551), Nikols¬kaya Church, and Uspensky Cathedral. When Alexander Pushkin first saw Sviyazhsk, he was overjoyed. It seems the city was exactly what he imagined for an ideal fairytale setting: beautiful island on a tall mountain, located exactly in the middle of a great river. This island with its surprising history cannot be found anywhere else in the world.

Elabuga This charming 1000 year old trade center that located on the shore of the river Kama and surrounded by natural beauty is one of the oldest cities in Tatarstan. Throughout its history the city was the cradle of Russian trade, where diverse waves of remarkable people flowed together. Most of its buildings have been preserved in their original condition to this day. Examples include the memorial house museum of Ivan Shishkin and the homestead museum of N. Durova, a famous heroine of the Fatherland War of 1812.

Tragic circumstances led the city to become the last refuge of the poet Maria Tsvetaeva. Not far from the Elabuga is the famous Elabuga mound "Chertovo gorodishe" the remains of a fortified settlement from the Volga tribes of the first millennium B.C. The surviving stone tower is a symbol of Elabuga. On the banks of the river Toima, five kilometers from Elabuga, archaeologists discovered the Ananinsky burial ground, which lends its name to an entire Iron Age culture.

<u>Kysh-Babay Residence (Tatar Santa Clause)</u> The residences of Kysh Babay and Kar Kyzy are located in the village of Yana Kyrlay, in a pine forest on the bank of the river Iya, 60 kilometers from Kazan. The fairytale journey begins with the forest "customs" where Shaitan leads you into the estate of Kysh Babay. The map of Shurale leads guests to path filled with adventures. Among the tales, mysteries, miracles, and fairytale characters you will meet Shurale (the Wood goblin), Shaitan (the Devil), Uburly Karchyk (the Witch), Azhdaha (the Dragon), Batyr (the Kinught), Altynchech (Goldilocks), Tahir and Zuhra (Romeo and Juliet).

<u>Chistopol</u> The historic town of Chistopol was founded in the 18th century. This town is truly a living museum, with streets and buildings that preserve the spirit of past days. A walk around Chistopol introduces you to the quiet, very special beauty of the Russian countryside. The Melnikov

House, the grounds of Uspensky Monastery, St. Nicholas Cathedral these places all enhance the feeling that the city was built with care and love. You can find very interesting Boris Pasternak museum here. A few kilometers from Chistopol you'll find the remains of Juketau, a city of the ancient Bolgar Kingdom which served as a trade center during pre-Mongol period.

<u>Tetushi</u> The pearl of Tetushi is historico-architectural natural park "Dolgaya polyana". Tourists visited this place say that you feel peace and calm. Local people claim there is anomalous zone with positive energy. Even Khans of Ancient Bolgar used to come to this place for several days to recover peace of mind. There are a lot of old buildings, dated from 1700th. You can even be lucky to see real archaeological excavation! And of course you can enjoy beautiful and splendid nature of Tetushi. Fond of historical reconstructions?

Then summer reconstruction of battlefield on Vshiha mountain is definitely worth visiting! You can not only watch, but also participate!

<u>Laishevo</u> When you will plan your visit to Tatarstan, please note, that in the end of May there is a big ethnic festival Karavon. For nine years annually more than 10 thousand people come to take part. And according to legend, this festival exists more than 300 years! Here you can dance in a round, have a look at the town of craftsman, take part in national amusements and feel cheerful and holiday atmosphere among wearing national costumes people. This festival is definitely worth seeing!

Detailed Guide to Kazan

Sightseeing in Kazan what to see. Complete travel guide

Kazan is a very contrasting city, which combines original Russian cultural traditions and Tatar mentality. Many visiting Russians feel themselves to be foreigners in Kazan, because Tatar is widely spoken in the city. Local people piously respect the ancient traditions and do not forget about their origin. At the same time, Kazan is part of Russia, and this fact is also treated with due respect.

The exact date of the foundation of the city is unknown, but its age is for sure more than a thousand years. The official date of the founding of the city is 1005, but new archaeological findings indicate that Kazan is exactly several dozen years older. The Kazan Kremlin is the main city landmark, which was built during the reign of Ivan the Terrible. It was built by Smolensk masters, who at that time were considered the best masons.

Kazan is a city of two world religions; along with Orthodox churches there are many mosques. Religious buildings are rightfully considered to be city's decorations. Among the sights of Kazan, the leaning tower is of special interest, with which is connected a beautiful legend about the Kazan queen. According to legend, Queen Syuyumbike was so beautiful that no one could resist her beauty. She was conquered by Ivan the Terrible himself, who sent her matchmakers. The queen, who hated the terrible Russian tsar, said that she would marry him only if he built a tower in a week. When the messengers of Ivan the Terrible met the deadline, Syuyumbike climbed to the top of the tower and threw herself down from it, only to not belong to the Russian Tsar.

Also, Kazan surprises with the location of the smallest subway in Europe located here. Inside the metro does not look diminutive: there are spacious vestibules, modern escalators, and many other things that were done counting on a large flow of tourists and locals. But there are only five metro stations in Kazan, and therefore locals prefer to travel to other destinations by other forms of public transport. The famous Kazan University operates in the city, and therefore a significant part of its residents are students. The favorite place for students to relax is the benches near the university, located in a semicircle; the locals call them a "frying pan". Here youths likes to gather, and often play songs with a guitar.

Kazan is one of richest Russian cities in attractions. The main historical symbol of the city is the Kazan Kremlin. This architectural complex includes constructions of the 12th-20th centuries. It is unique because its exterior amazingly combines Western and Eastern traditions. Near the Orthodox temple, you can see an incredibly beautiful mosque. There is the Turkic tower near luxurious mansions in European style. It is just impossible to look over all the Kremlin attractions in just one day.

Another interesting attraction is the Temple of All Religions. This religious monument has a lot of architectural peculiarities. The author of this unusual temple's project was the humanist Ildar Hasanov. He managed to create the project of the temple that combines 16 confessions. The construction is a difficult asymmetrical complex with domes and towers in all the colors of the rainbow. On the facade, you can see windows of different shape and size, arches, and other unusual decorative elements. Since its construction, no religious events have been held in this temple. It has only an architectural value.

The Palace of Farmers has a special value among architectural monuments of Kazan. With its exterior, it resembles luxurious palaces built in the period between the 18th-19th centuries in Italy. Actually, this luxurious building was built not so long ago, in 2010. Today, this belongs to the Ministry of Agriculture of Tatarstan. The temple is surrounded by the beautiful landscape garden.

Another historical monument is Shamil's House. This beautiful mansion was built in the 19th century. The family of the famous imam Shamil lived here. At the beginning of the 20th century, this historical building was almost destroyed in a fire but then was reconstructed fast. After the Revolution of 1917, all the values were withdrawn out of the mansion and it was rebuilt into the house. People had lived here until 1981. In 1986, the mansion was turned into the museum dedicated to the works of the famous poet Gabdulla Tukai.

Near it, there is another luxurious monument of the early 20th century, Ushakov's House. This mansion was built by the famous merchant Alexey Ushakov for his bride. Since its construction and up to this day, the house is considered as one of the most beautiful in Kazan.

Cuisine & restaurants

Cuisine of Kazan for gourmets. Places for dinner best restaurants

Rest in Kazan is simply impossible to imagine without visiting popular restaurants, this city has embodied all the best traditions of the national Tatar cuisine. Tatars who lived on the territory of Russia, early began to engage in sedentary farming and livestock, and that is why meat, dairy and flour dishes became the basis of national cuisine.

Initially, the most important dishes of national cuisine were broths and soups. Later, various vegetable dishes took a worthy place in national cuisine, but soups with flour dressing are still a daily dish in any family. Gourmets certainly should try tokamach and noodles soup cooked on classic recipes; this is one of the most delicious national treats. The basis of the second dishes is potatoes and vegetables. Often as a second dish boiled meat is served, and the broth is used for making other treats. Usually boiled meat is a little stewed in oil with pepper and vegetables; it turns out incredibly tasty and juicy.

In addition to meat, regular boiled potatoes with horseradish are often served, a significant part of the national treats are simple to cook. On holidays, one of the main dishes is a chicken stuffed with eggs and milk. Considering the fact that the dough plays an important role in the national cuisine of the Tatar people, there are also a lot of pies baked here; local hostesses are able to cook hundreds of different types of dough. The most ancient of all existing pies is "kystybai" a combination of mashed potatoes, millet porridge and unleavened dough.

A fairly common treat is a "balish" cake, which is made from unleavened dough, and as a filling, pieces of lamb, ducklings or goose with the addition of potatoes is used. This popular cake is made both large and small. If we talk about sweets, the real symbol of the Tatar cuisine is the "chak-chak". In appearance, it is a bit like a pie but chak-chak is prepared with the addition of fragrant honey. In addition to it, it is customary to serve fragrant herbal tea. In Kazan there are excellent restaurants, which serve Tatar cuisine. Very popular restaurants are "Bilyar", "House of Tatar Cooking", "Alan-Ashe" and "Azu". Popular pastries can be tried not only in a restaurant or cafe; it is sold literally in all local supermarkets.

Bahetle Supermarket

This is actually a chain of grocery stores, but they also have their own kitchen where they cook lots of healthy Russian and Tatar food from meat, fish, vegetables and so on. It's especially popular around businessmen who don't have time for cooking, so they just come over and pick up the ready dinner.

Here you can also find lots of different pies (not everything is super tasty but they have some good stuff). The store is opened from 8 a.m. till 11 p.m. (If you come early in the morning you can get really fresh home-made bread and cakes). There are many Bahetles around the city, but this one is the most centrally located.

Location
Bahetie Supermarket
8, Ershova street
Kazan

Bilar Restaurant

A good alternative to DTK as it also has a very tasty Tatar cuisine but for lower prices. The interior is made in Eastern style, so you can feel the national atmosphere.

The highlight of the restaurant are the comfortable chairs with the requisite multi-colored cushions and cushion covers that look like they were sourced from a dodgy Turkish carpet salesman.

Here you would probably find younger people than rich businessmen like in DTK or Pashmir. Average bill here is 1200 rubles (€25).

Location
Bilar Restaurant
31, Butlerova street
Kazan
Phone: +7 843 264-65-65

DTK Restaurant
Specialized on Tatar cuisine, this restaurant lacks cozy, intimate atmosphere, but makes up for it with a professional service and a wide range of

options on the menu. Decorated in somewhat pompous style, the restaurant features dishes from the Tatar diaspora around the world. Average bill is 2000 R (€50), but be prepared to spend more if you decide to go all the way and bring yourself to food coma.

Location
DTK Restaurant
31/12, Baumana street
Kazan
Phone: +7 (843) 292-70-70

Dobraya Stolovaya Canteen
The motto of Dobraya Stolovaya canteen promises that tasty doesn't necessary mean expensive and in this case it is hard to argue with that.

Here you can get e.g. simple and nutritious breakfasts every Russian kid was getting in a school canteen for 43 RUB (less than €1). This offer is valid from 7-30 to 11 am.

Location

Dobraya Stolovaya Canteen
21, Baumana street, 2 floor
Kazan

Kazan Central Market
The culture of street markets is very developed in Kazan, although it is already becoming replaced by European supermarkets. Kazan Central Market is the most accessible and gives you a good idea of the atmosphere of the real Tatar bazar. Here you can find everyting for very cheap prices fruit, vegetables, dairy products and meat , as well as some delicious, locally made treats. A walk around the stalls seeing what's on the offer is an experience in itself. It's also a good chance to discover the Russia of the 90s, as almost nothing changed in the market since then. Open 8.00 17.00 except Mondays.

Location
Kazan Central Market
13, Martyna Mezhlauka
Kazan

Culture: sights to visit

Culture of Kazan. Places to visit old town, temples, theaters, museums and palaces

The sights of Kazan amaze with its magnificence and diversity, among which is an old building of the Kazan railway station, located in the heart of the city. Equally beautiful are the ancient temples of the Zilantov Monastery, and the panorama of the Kazanka River which can be admired for hours. The snow-white walls of the Kazan Kremlin, behind which the domes of churches and minarets of mosques are hardly visible, are the main historical symbol of the city and the most important landmark of the region. Thousand-year-old Kazan can truly impress the imagination with its architectural and historical monuments, of which there are a great many.

In the historical center, various styles and structures peacefully coexist, both of the Tatar pattern and of the original Russian. The modern part of the city is well-equipped. It is famous for its numerous entertainment centers, parks and sports complexes. Along with Kremlin, important features of the historical appearance of Kazan are numerous religious monuments. Here is located the Qolsarif mosque the largest mosque in Europe.

There are excellent observation platforms on the territory of the Kremlin, from which a very picturesque view of the banks of the Volga opens, especially in the place where Kazanka flows into it. Here is an island on which a monument to Russian soldiers, who died during the capture of Kazan, was built. Previously, the monument was called "The Temple of Holy Face of Christ the Savior". Bauman Street, which is secretly called "Kazansky Arbat", is located in the center of the city, among its main decorations, the Epiphany Cathedral, in which Feodor Chaliapin was christened.

The bizarre bell tower of the cathedral is considered the most interesting decoration of the historic street, to which leads six bridges, which cross over the Bulaq canal. Each of the bridges not only has its own name, but also its own history. Despite the fact that the bridges are already several centuries old, they are perfectly preserved and manage their destination.

If you go to one of the old lanes from Bauman Street, you can go to Kazan University; it is one of the largest educational centers in Russia. In addition to the university itself, the most beautiful buildings of the National Museum, the National Library and the Alexandrovsky Passage are located in this area. In Kazan, there are many interesting places and attractions; there are chic architectural monuments, traces of ancient majestic cities, monasteries and mosques. To see at least half of the outstanding sights of the city, you need to visit here more than once

Tatar State Academic Theatre of Opera and Ballet
Tatarstan's spiritual home of opera and ballet, this grand theatre was built in 1851, although the company's history dates back further to 1791. Their repertoire includes many international favourites such Aida, Giselle, Carmen, the Magic Flute and Rigoletto as well as numerous Russian classics such as Boris Godunov, Sleeping Beauty, Eugene Onegin and Anyuta. Watch out also for performances of the home grown opera Jalil which tells the story of the local hero and poet who fought with partisan troops behind enemy lines during World War II.

Kazan Arena
Ever wondered where the largest outside screen in Europe was? Wonder no more. The Kazan Arena is a futuristic sporting complex in the Tatar capital,

with a capacity of 45,379. The stadium looks like a water lily from the sky, although it is unlikely any fans will get to see that.

Getting there: There are plenty of public transport options for getting to the Kazan Arena, but access will change on game day. Passengers will be let off at Veterinarnaya Akademiya (accessed by bus lines 10, 18, 33, 35, 35A, 36, 44, 45, 46, 49, 55, 60 and 62, or tram number 5) or at the intersection of Adoratsky Street and Yamasheva Prospect, accessed either by a plethora of buses (33, 46, 49, 60, 10A, 15, 18, 35, 35A, 36, 44, 45, 62, 76) or tram 5. Shuttle buses will also run from Kazan's train stations and airport.

Galiaskar Kamal State Academic Theatre
Tartarstan's leading theatre and one of the most popular theatres in the whole country. Yes the plays are performed in the Tatar language, but it's ok! Every seat has headphones where you can

listen to Russian or English translations. During the Soviet era Tatarstan was not allowed its own film studios and so theatre became the only way for actors to perform hence the performances here are of consistently high quality.

Attractions & nightlife

City break in Kazan. Active leisure ideas for Kazan attractions, recreation and nightlife
Night life in Kazan is very diverse. As in any major city, there are many nightclubs that offer an entertainment program for every taste. There are clubs for people who prefer not to spend a lot of money on vacation, and there are clubs for those who like to have fun from the heart. There are many themed clubs in Kazan. Lovers of evening entertainment should pay attention to the clubs "Goa", "De-ja-vu", "Louis 13" and "Garage".

Rest in the beautiful modern city will appeal not only to fans of incendiary parties, but also to those who like to spend time outdoors. The main natural landmark of the city is the beautiful river Kazanka, on the shore of which several beautiful recreation areas are fitted. In the warm season you can swim and sunbathe, and during the off-season scenic spots are perfect for picnics and hiking. For walking tours, the Victory Park, as well as the picturesque Tatarstan Street, which is decorated with luxurious fountains, is perfect.

There is an excellent water park "Riviera" in the city, which occupies a vast territory and is ready to offer visitors a wide variety of entertainment. For admirers of serene leisure, there are huge pools with sun terraces, and for fans of outdoor activities there are many slides and attractions. More quiet and secluded is the water park Baryonix. Here you can comfortably relax even with young children.

For those who have a merry holiday associated with modern shopping and entertainment complexes, it is worth visiting the center of Park House. In addition to a huge number of specialized stores and luxury boutiques, it is the site of the modern cinema "Kinoplex", as well as one of the most popular bowling centers of the city. Also in the center there are about ten attractive cafes and restaurants.

In the center of Kazan is the entertainment complex Suvar Plaza, which is characterized by an incredibly beautiful design. There are spacious cavaedum, colorful recreation areas for young guests and dozens of different shops for every taste and purse. The entertainment area includes a state-of-the-art Grand Cinema, first-class cafes and bars. Sports lovers and gourmets will like the "Bahetle" center more, where one of the best sports bars in the city is located and an excellent restaurant of oriental cuisine.

Tips for tourists

Preparing your trip to Kazan: advices & hints things to do and to obey

1. At the Kazan railway station, cash desks always have large queues, where you can stand for hours. It is best to book tickets on the website of the Russian Railways. The price will be exactly the same, and the time saving is undeniable. You can pay for this ticket using an electronic card or mobile phone.

2. For tourists who are staying at Kazan airport, it will be easier and cheaper to get to the city center by bus number 97. Those who decide to use taxi services will have to pay an order of magnitude more.

3. The most important landmark of the city is the Kazan Kremlin located a couple of minutes walk from the railway station. Visiting this landmark of world significance is worth it even to those travelers who will be passing through Kazan.

4. On the Kremlin street is the main information center, where you can confirm the schedule of public transport, the time of cultural events, the location of interesting sites and everything that is so important for active tourists.

5. The most popular form of public transport is buses, and also on the territory of the city you can comfortably move on trolleybuses and trams. There is also a modern metro in Kazan, but due to the short length of the line it does not enjoy popularity among locals.

6. Travelers expecting to bring a lot of interesting souvenirs from the trip should definitely pay

attention to luxurious velvet dressing gowns, painted utensils and handmade products made of wood, as well as skullcaps and leather goods souvenirs in the "Tatar style" will be the best option .

7. The hotel infrastructure of Kazan continues to improve. Today the city presents hotels and guesthouses of various categories. Economical tourists should pay attention not only to classical cheap hotels, but also to mini-hotels, they are distinguished by pleasant prices and high level of equipment.

8. There are many adherents of the Muslim faith in the city, in connection with which it is worth observing certain rules. Going for a walk around the city or sightseeing, you should choose classic clothes, and extravagant outfits are best reserved for a more suitable occasion.

Places in Kazan

It's easy to confuse Kazan with Kazahstan (hello Borat!) orKazantip (sorry, no crazy parties on the beach here). In fact Kazanis one of the biggest Russian cities (1.2 million people live there) and it's the capital of Tatarstan Republic, one of the most developed areas in Russia.

Kazan is probably the most tourist-friendly city in Russia after St. Petersburg. It's clean, safe, relaxed, rich, and has lots of beautiful sights and places to chill. The special thing about Kazan is the mix of two cultures: East and West, Muslim and Orthodox.

here are not many places in the world where such a diverse population cohabits in such a peaceful manner and Kazan is a great example of that. Kazan is also one of the oldest Russian city (older than Moscow), in 2005 it celebrated its millennium birthday.

Back in the days it used to be the capital of powerful Khanate of Kazanafter the fall of Golden Horde. In 1552 the city was conquered by the forces of Ivan the Terrible. During the next years this region had been settled by Russians, and native population, Tatars, were massacred or forcibly Christianized. Now the population of Kazan is mixed, but stillTatars make up about 43% of the city's population and maintain their own language and traditions.

People are proud of their culture and try to save it, which is also encouraged on the state level. For example, Tatar language is official; all students must learn it at school. All signs in Kazan are written both in Russian and Tatar. It is more common to see the Tatar flag than the Russian flag. You will probably find here more mosques, than churches.

So, it can hardly remind a typical Russian city, what makes it much more interesting in this sense. Recently Kazan was granted the status of the "third capital of Russia". In some ways that's true. It's a rich industrial city, cultural and educational centre. Kazan federal university is the second oldest university in Russia.

Now Kazan is actively trying to become a sport capital of the country as well. Every football fan knows "Rubin Kazan" and hockey lovers know "Ak Bars". In July 2013 it hosted Universiade (Student Olympic Games) and in 2018 there will be FIFA World Cup in Kazan. That means that the concentration of money in Kazan is increasing and it's becoming more developed and beautified for travelers with every year.

Temple of All Religions

This Russian religious complex is a Frankenstein's chapel that includes influence from almost all the major faiths.

Located in the Russian city of Kazan, the colorful Temple of All Religions, or Universal Temple is a mish-mash of architectural flourishes culled from most of the major world religions to create an uber-complex where all religions can come together in harmony.

Established by philanthropist Ildar Khanov in 1992, the site is not actually a chapel in the traditional sense but is instead a center meant to stand as a symbol of religious unity. Khanov was an active proponent of rehabilitation services and, having overseen a few in his lifetime, built the center with the help of patients he met through his work.

The exterior of the Temple looks almost like something out of a Disneyland Small World display, with a Greek Orthodox dome here and a Russian minaret there. There are influences culled from Jewish synagogues and Islamic mosques, and a number of spires and bells. All said the Temple incorporates architectural influences from 16 separate religions in a bright cacophony of devotion.

Khanov and his assistants lived at the site, working continually on the construction until Khanov's death in 2013. Today the Temple is still not freely open to the public but Khanov's associates still live on site and continue his work on the center.

Know Before You Go
You can reach the temple from Kazan by bus number 2 (leaves from railway station). Part of the building has been recently damaged by fire, but some rooms of the complex are open to visit. In June 2018, the temple was actually open and a ticket cost about 50 roebel.

Qolşärif Mosque

Replica of mosque destroyed by Russia in the 16th century.

In Northwestern Russia, a Disney-like castle seems to magically appear in the town of Kazan. In a passing glance, it seems more like a princess' legendary palace, but the minarets with crescent moons signal something very different.

In the 16th Century prior to the invasion of Kazan a mosque stood here which was named after its leading teacher Qol Sharif. Qol Sharif died alongside his students trying to save the mosque from the Tsar's forces, but unfortunately it was destroyed in 1522 and for centuries the site remained empty. Following the fall of the Soviet Union, with the help of many other counties including Saudi Arabia and UAE, the mosque was rebuilt, albeit in a modern style.

The impressive new mosque was finally inaugurated in 2005 when Kazan celebrated its millennium and now stands as a prominent symbol of the city, rightly recognised as one of Kazan's most worthy sights as well as Europe's largest mosque. The Qol Sharif largely functions as a museum although thousands of Muslims do gather here to pray on major religious holidays.

Qolşärif Mosque was first constructed in the 16th century in the Muslim-dominated Khanate of Kazan. The people were decidedly different from ethnic Russians, and spoke the Tatar language and practiced Islam. Qolşärif was a massive place of worship in the town and was famed to be the largest mosque in Europe. Built early in the 16th century, the Mosque was a symbol of Tatar strength in the era.

Unfortunately, Ivan the Terrible was gaining power throughout Russia, and eventually came to claim a toll from Kazan. In 1552, he stormed the city and destroyed the monumental mosque. After its fall, Kazan was swept into the larger Russian state, although the Tatar architecture was not all lost in the coming change. Some claim that Qolşärif's soaring minarets influenced St. Basil's Cathedral, where construction began only three years after the fall of Kazan.

In 1996, a project began in Kazan to rebuild the Qolşärif Mosque as true to form as possible. Funded partly by Saudi Arabia and the United Arab Emirates, the final project was finished in 2005 and is a splendid wonder. With soaring teal-topped minarets and whitewashed arches, the new mosque connects the old Kazan Khanate with modern Russian and Islamic architecture, and serves to keep the memory of the 16th century mosque alive.

Soviet Lifestyle Museum

This nostalgic Russian museum is full of USSR cultural artifacts from the 1970s and 80s.
While there is much about life under the Iron Curtain that was despicable and unfortunate, that doesn't mean that there wasn't culture, even if it was fraught with propaganda and misinformation. The Soviet Lifestyle Museum explores the USSR's musical, educational, and yes, propagandistic days of yore.

Kitsch isn't the first thing that comes to mind when people talk about the old USSR, but at the Soviet Lifestyle Museum, it's king. Held in a former communal apartment that would have been home to 20 some people, the little museum is now home to a collection that has items from time periods ranging from the 1930s to the 1990s, focusing on a few distinct aspects of Soviet life.

One portion of the exhibit focuses on the high school experience, and claims to be one of the most comprehensive collections on the subject in existence. There is also a gallery that displays a collection of Soviet-era artwork, and a selection of propaganda books. However maybe the strangest aspect of the museum is the section dedicated to the influence of rock-and-roll in the Soviet Union. With a collection of around 60 guitars signed by artists ranging from Sting to Scorpions, it shines a light on the influence of Western music in the culture of the time.

There is also a rack of clothes that guests are welcome to try on and take pictures in. Because if you are going to travel back to the Soviet 80s, it's pics or it didn't happen.

Know Before You Go

Take Universitetskaya to Ostrovskogo. The museum is on the corner. Go upstairs.

Suyumbike Tower

Russia's own leaning tower was built on a tragic historical fable.

Suyumbike Tower in the Kazan Kremlin is a gorgeous piece of historic Russian architecture with a tragic story in its past and a growing slant in its future.

Kazan's very own leaning tower. The striking 55 metre high tower with a slight lean is heavily associated with a legend surrounding Princess Soyembika, one of the last great rulers of Kazan. According to the legend Ivan the Terrible proposed marriage to the beautiful leader, but she refused him and so Ivan instead decided to lay siege to her city. After much destruction she finally relented and agreed to marry the Tsar but only if he proved his worthiness by building her a seven storey tower within a week. After seven days the Tsar's workers had completed the task and so Soyembika reluctantly climbed to the top of the tower, took one last look over her city and leapt to her death.

Of course the dramatic tale is purely legend. Soyembika was in fact taken by the Tsars guards during the siege and forced into exile where she eventually died alone. The true origins of the tower are still shrouded in mystery however and some scholars claim that the tower may date back to before Ivan the Terrible's invasion of Kazan, while others claim it was built following the Tsar's conquering of the city. If the tower looks familiar then you are probably being reminded of Moscow's Kazan station, whose design was inspired by it. Unfortunately the tower can only be admired from the outside.

According to legend, after Ivan the Terrible seized Kazan, he wanted to celebrate by taking the deposed Khan's niece, Suyumbike, as his bride. The beautiful Princess Suyumbike initially refused, saying she would only agree to marry him if he could build a tower higher than either of them had ever seen. The conquering Tsar did just that, erecting the spire in just six days. After it was completed, Suyumbike said she wanted to look out upon the city from the high tower. When she reached the top however, the princess jumped to her death. Ivan may have taken the city but he could never have Suyumbike's heart.

Despite the dramatic origin story the tower was not actually constructed until at least 100 years after Ivan's conquest of Kazan in 1552. Consisting of six widening tiers built on a gated arch, the 58-meter baked brick tower stands as Kazan's most iconic building. The actual age of the tower is unknown as all relevant documents were destroyed in a fire, but it is likely that the tower was built as part of a strengthening of the Kremlin's defenses in the early 18th century in response to multiple rebellions. In recent years the tower's weak foundation has begun to sink giving the tower a noticeable lean that will likely become more dramatic in the coming years.

The entire Kazan Kremlin was declared a UNESCO World Heritage site in 2000, and Suyumbike Tower is easily the most iconic of the now protected buildings. Despite the tragic love story behind this tower, the world's love affair with the site isn't ending any time soon.

Raifa Monastery

The Raifa Monastery of the Kazan eparchy is situated about 27 km north-west from Kazan. It was founded in the early XVII century and became a very important pilgrimage direction for the Orthodox Christians: the believers from all over the country come there to pray for the Georgian icon of Godmother a copy from the very first icon originated from the Krasnogorsky Monastery (close to Kholmogory). This cloister was built on the territory which since olden times had been pagan and later, Islamic and became one of the earliest Orthodox monasteries appeared there after the Siege of Kazan (1552).

Museum of 1000 years of Kazan

It's an awful long walk all the way out to this new museum (if you are getting cold and tired hop on any of the buses heading up the hill and get off at the theatre), housed in the Kazan National Cultural Centre. However along the way you will gain a real insight into the city's growth as you pass the many beautiful historic old buildings and imaginative new ones which make up this diplomatic area of the city. This museum was built to honour Kazan's millennial birthday in 2005 and a collection of ancient artifacts, scriptures, pictures and maps trace the city's history. Behind the museum is a great view out over the Kazanka river.

House of Zinaida Ushkova

House of Zinaida Ushkova (Vysotskaya) daughter of a professor of surgery and wife of an owner of chemical plants and a tea magnate is a splendid mansion in the centre of Kazan built in 1904 1908 in the eclectic style by the architect Karl Müfke. Since 1919 it is the head building of the National Library of the Republic of Tatarstan, however not everyone knows that the interiors of the house are definitely worth of visiting.

Each room as well as the fabulous *Chinoiserie* (Chinese alike) staircase were designed in its own unique style, and you can literally learn the history of art styles just by walking through the rooms of the mansion. Gothic, Napoleon-empire, Baroque, Rococo, Moresque, Arabic... the list might be continued.

One of the main attractions is the reading room transformed into an exotic garden with evergreen plants and streamy fountains. What a perfect place to relax with a book!

Peter and Paul Cathedral

Decorated in the so-called Naryshkin style, this beautiful 18th Century cathedral was built to commemorate Peter the Great's visit to the city in 1722. Featuring a vibrant and distinctive exterior decoration the roofs are covered in bright blue and white tiling while the peachy walls are decorated with bright baroque floral patterns it's a rare example of the Russian baroque movement. The lower chapel based in the tower was used in the winter (it is smaller and has no windows). The upper part of the church (reached by climbing the steep stone staircase) has tall ceilings and unusually for an Orthodox church windows which let in a special ethereal light effect at certain times of day. The highlight of the cathedral is its huge iconostasis covered in precious metals and stones and the view over the town from the top of the church steps.

Blagoveshchensky Cathedral

Erected between 1556 and 1562, this is Kazan's most important cathedral and the home of the holiest copy of the Our Lady of Kazan icon, which was presented to the city by Pope John Paul II in 2005. The cathedral, which was built in a style similar to that of the Assumption cathedral in the Moscow Kremlin, was destroyed many times by fire over the centuries and following the Bolshevik revolution it suffered yet more damage as the Soviets destroyed the bell tower and other ecclesiastical buildings which surrounded it.

In the 1990s concerted restoration work began and in summer 2005 the cathedral once again began to accept worshipers as it returned to its function as a working place of worship. The interior painting and iconostasis are mostly modern although many of the icons which were donated to the cathedral date back centuries. Be sure to pass behind the Cathedral to admire the spectacular view over the river.

Bolgar State Historical and Architectural Reserve

Located some 140km away from Kazan itself, this is exactly what it claims to be. A UNESCO World Heritage Site, it is evidence of the medieval city of

Bolgar, an Islamic stronghold that served as a capital of the Golden Horde in the 13th century. Two buses head this way from Kazan every day, with the journey lasting two and a half hours.

Old Tatar Village

After the Siege of Kazan (1552) the tatars had to move to the village behind the city wall. The unique ensemble of Tatar residential and religious architecture was formed in the 17-18th centuries. There you can visit the Märcani Mosque one of the oldest mosque in Kazan (ul. Kayuma Nasyri 17) built in 1766-1770-s, the museum of the great Tatar poet Gabdulla Tukay (ul. Gabdully Tukaya 74) and the Galiaskar Kamal State Academic Theatre (ul. Tatarstan 1).

Best Things to Do in Kazan, Russia

Kazan, a city deriving its name from the Tatar word for cooking pot, is true to its name. Over a hundred years older than Moscow, a genuine stew of both Tatar and Slavic cultures makes the capital of the Tatarstan Republic a treasure to explore. Here are 10 recommendations for what to do in Kazan that will ensure you get the most out of the city.

Immerse yourself in the Middle Ages in the Kremlin
Many Russian cities started with the construction of a kremlin and Kazan is no exception. This is where you should start your tour of the city. It's the oldest building in the city and was rebuilt in the second half of the 16th century on Ivan the Terrible's orders. Postnik Yakovlev and Ivan Shiryai, the architects responsible for one of Moscow's most iconic symbols St. Basil's Cathedral were involved in the construction of the fortress.

Don't let Söyembikä Tower topple

According to legend, the tower is named after the only woman to rule the Kazan Khanate. Ivan the Terrible heard of Söyembikä's beauty and proposed to her, but she turned him down so the Russian tsar threatened to raze Kazan to the ground. Söyembikä had to agree to marry him, but in return she asked for an unusual wedding present: A seven-storey tower to be built in seven days. Her desire was fulfilled and the tower was built one floor a day. On day seven the tower was completed and the wedding feast started. During the celebrationSöyembikä climbed the tower and threw herself off it.

It's situated in the grounds of the Kazan Kremlin. Its height is 58 meters and as of today it leans by two meters, like the famous Leaning Tower of Pisa

Taste Tatar cuisine
Echpochmak, smetannik, peremyach, bokkan, and baursak you must try these! To appreciate real

homemade Tatar cuisine and a Soviet ambiance at the same time, you can go to the Tea House at 64 Bauman Street. The place is indeed reminiscent of a Soviet canteen, but the locals are fond of it and many come here for lunch.

Admire the architecture of the Palace of Farmers
This building proudly calls itself a "palace" and attracts tourists from all over the world. The Palace of Farmers houses the Ministry of Agriculture but not all locals appreciate its splendor: Activists campaigned against the modern Baroque Revival style during its construction from 2008-10. Some people think it's tasteless and ugly. What do you think?

See the sunset from Kremlin Embankment
If you go through the park adjacent to the Palace of Farmers, you'll end up on the Kremlin Embankment. The best time to come here is in the

evening. And if you're lucky, you might catch one of the most fantastic sunsets you are likely to see.

See Kazan at night from the other bank
The Kazan Family Center, which is also a registry office, is situated on the other side on the River Kazanka. According to legend, the name of the city comes from the word "kazan" which means a "cauldron," and the building really does resemble a big cooking pot, symbolizing abundance and fertility. Along its perimeter the Kazan Center is guarded by winged leopards and Zilant dragons. Thirty-two meters up on the eighth floor there's a platform that offers a panoramic view of the city's historic part. The view is particularly beautiful after sunset: All of the Kremlin buildings and the embankment are illuminated and the lights are reflected in the river.

Ride the metro

The Kazan underground is very small one line and 10 stations but in beauty it is well nigh on a par with the legendary Moscow Metro thanks to its unique frescoes and mosaics on the walls, stained-glass windows, and huge amount of marble in its cladding. By the way, the tokens that are used for travel on the underground are also available as souvenirs.

What to do in Kazan for families with children

Kazan is a great place you can confidently visit with your family and children, without any risks of boredom during the trip. From the «city of professions» and scientific and entertainment centres, to the planetarium and interactive museums, Kazan has a lot to offer for its younger visitors and their families. Let us give you a glimpse into just some of the places that can help entertain, feed and cheer up your young travelers

KidSpace

Inside the KidSpace "city of professions" amusement park, children can realize their dreams of a potential future career. For a short period of time, let your child step into the shoes of a scientist, doctor, traveler, artist or one of the many other careers set out among the 20 "workplaces". Here, young journalists are taught to conduct interviews, and bakers and confectioners have an opportunity to bake cookies and pizza.

Upon entering the new world, your child receives a passport of a "KidSpace" city resident and a cheque, which can be exchanged for "experiences" in the "bank". "Experiences" are this city's currency that are spent on acquiring new skills, entertainment and games. Any unused "experiences" can be stored in their own "bank account" and used during their next visit.

Zarnitsa
In the scientific-entertainment centre for children aged 2 to 14 years old, there are several themed locations: the "Safe City", "City of Masters", "Naukograd" ("Science-city"), "Cosmodrome", "Defender of the Motherland", "Applied Art", and "Academy of Talents". In "Zarnitsa", children are taught how to build a fire, start a car, draw complex pictures and navigate the stars, and if that's not enough, they can also sign up to master classes, where they will learn more about science and art.

If your child is over 7 years of age, you can let them play and learn here freely under the watchful eye of the staff while you enjoy a cup of coffee, go on a tour of the stadium or play squash.

Kazan Circus

The Kazan circus makes it seem as if a UFO has "landed" at the Kremlin's doorstep. Its outer appearance alone is enough to attracts the attention of children.

Inside, everything is as it should be an orchestra under the dome, a red arena with spectators scattered around it. The lamps in the foyer look like balloons, and the staircase leading to the second floor resembles a giraffe. During performance days, a children's railway train operates within the building. It is worthwhile to go here, even if it's just to hold your breath as you watch the deadly acrobatic tricks, laugh with the clowns, and see the world's tallest brown bear and predatory animals perhaps the main stars of the program

Planetarium

A visit to the planetarium is an exciting adventure for any child. The equipment installed here allows you to take a look into other galaxies, inspect the Sun and other stars, or take a trip to the most remote corners of the universe. In the foyer of the planetarium you'll find an exhibition that visually shows the effect of gravity, shares stories about the life of astronauts and other interesting facts. With the help of the dome ceiling, children will be shown a starry sky from different points of the Earth and will have an opportunity to compare our galaxy with other planetary systems. For those who want to learn a little more, the planetarium staff also conduct interactive tours.

On your way back, after a fun-filled afternoon, don't miss the Engelhardt Astronomical Observatory, built in 1899 located next door to the planetarium.

Museum of Natural History of Tatarstan

This museum will become a real treasure trove for children interested in animals, plants and minerals. It is remarkable not only for its wealth of exhibits, but also for the modern multimedia equipment: touch-screen kiosks, monitors and plasma screen panels, which are an interesting and fascinating way to learn about the rich flora and fauna of the region.

The museum contains a lot of interactive elements a particular favourite of many is the "space scales" that will show you your weight on the Moon, Mars and other planets of the solar system.

City Panorama" Exhibition Complex

This museum is a sure way to spend both an entertaining and educational afternoon, because of the truly interactive format in which the history of the millennial city is presented here. The "City Panorama" issues hand held electronic tablets that will serve as a guide for visitors to travel through the four buildings of the museum as you learn about the history of Kazan from ancient times to present day.

On the round screen with a video panorama, you'll be able to watch historical short films about Kazan, and on the big screen see the city from a bird's eye view. Particularly noteworthy are two large model mockups of Kazan the winter of the 16th century and the summer of the 18th century. The mockups are not simple: the projector recreates the events of those times for example, the attack on Kazan by troops of Ivan the Terrible. Modern Kazan can also be viewed on a layout that is planned to be constantly updated alongside future changes of the city.

With the help of virtual reality technology, your child can take an exciting journey into the past to shake hands with Peter I, take a selfie with Tatar poet Gabdulla Tukay and become acquainted with other famous historical figures.

The museum has a children's room where kids of all ages are invited to take part in a game on the big screen, based on the story of an old legend about Kazan. In it, the brave batyr fights snakes and, after defeating them, goes in to battle the Zilant dragon.

At the end of your tour, don't miss a trip to the cafe which has been created to portray a 19th-20th century city tram. Embark on a virtual trip through historical Kazan, and rest and relax as you enjoy the national pastries and fragrant tea.

Lunchtime with Kids

Skazka
This is one of the oldest family businesses in the city a "children's cafe", which has been operating

since 1970. People of all ages come to this place for the legendary 1970s ice cream which is served in a "kremanka" ice cream dish from the Soviet era. It's hard not to feel like you are being transported back to your childhood while you're here. Other than ice cream, the menu contains a large selection of children's dishes: salads, cereals, soups, pastries and desserts made on the premises. "Skazka" are all about children here, the cafe contains a children's games room with a soft floor and toys, and even organizes regular culinary master classes.

Basilico
Lovers of Italian pizza should not miss the Basilico restaurant, located near the "Skazka" cafe. The pizzas are prepared under the guidance of one of the best pizzamakers of Naples, in an authentic stone pizza oven. Basilico is very welcoming of visitors with children and highchairs are provided if

need-be. Older children will also enjoy this place Basilico organizes master classes, where they have a chance to prepare their own pizza creations with the restaurant chef's guidance.

La Famiglia
An Italian restaurant is an excellent place for a family dinner. This one is located on the Kremlin embankment, from which you can enjoy a picturesque view of the new part of the city. The restaurant has a big menu for adults and children, as well as various cereals and soups for the youngest of guests. Children are also given the opportunity to learn to cook themselves on Sundays, the restaurant hosts culinary master classes where young participants are taught to cook pizza, which they can then enjoy themselves and treat their parents to a bite or two

Tour Russia's Most Unique Kremlin

One thing many travelers don't realize, if they've never visited Russia, is that there is no such thing as "The" Kremlin, though Moscow's usually gets the most attention. Every Russian city of a certain size has a Kremlin (which means "citadel" in Russian); they all feature a combination of government, religious and military buildings inside a wall, often over a body of water (the Volga River, in Kazan's case). The Kazan Kremlin has a decidedly Islamic character, owing to the city's large Muslim population and the mosque that exists within the citadel.

Experience All the World's Religions in One Building
Kazan has long gained accolades not only from within Russia, but from all around the world, for the fact the Christians and Muslims have lived together here in peace for nearly a millennium. Although it's easy to see this harmony lived out among locals, one site that pays homage to co-

existence is the aptly-named Temple of All Religions. This sacred site, which features multiple architectural styles in order to achieve its aim, sits just outside Kazan's city center.

...Or Many
Of course, you're welcome to appreciate Kazan's religious eclecticism in a more piecemeal fashion, if that suits you. Within the aforementioned Kazan Kremlin, for example, you'll find the blue-domed Kul Sharif Mosque, as well as the Anunciation Cathedral, which represents Russian Orthodox Christianity. Religious sites are abundant outside the Kremlin as well, from Marcani Mosque to St. Peter and Paul's Cathedral.

Relax in a Variety of Green Spaces
Kazan is well-known within Russia for the quality of life its citizens enjoy, and a big part of this is the wide variety of green spaces in the city. The most popular of these is Millennium Park, built to

commemorate the city's 1,000th birthday in 2005. Other Kazan Parks include the Central Park of Culture and Park Imeni.

Cool Off at an Exciting Water Park
Kazan is also home to a park of another sort, in the form of Riviera Aquapark. This park comes in handy too, since Kazan is much hotter than other cities in Russia, with summer temperatures that regularly rise into the '80s and '90s. A trip to Riviera Aquapark is a particularly good choice if you won't have the time to explore the lakes you find in Tatarstan outside Kazan.

Go Back in Time to the Soviet Union
hough Kazan was never a purely Russian city, it was nonetheless under the control of the Soviet Union during the country's entire existence. A stop at the quirky Soviet Lifestyle Museum is not so much a lesson in Soviet history (though there is plenty of artwork and other propaganda in case

that's your thing), but a compelling comparison of how things were under the USSR government vs today's largely autonomous regime.

Then, Participate Shamelessly in Capitalism

Like Moscow, Kazan is home to its own GUM department store, as well as a number of other "big box" retailers that would have Stalin rolling over in his grave. Heading to the more traditional Koltso shopping area, meanwhile, allows you to browse local Tatar handicrafts, including *Tubeteika* hats that are a common sight throughout Central Asia.

Get in the Festival Spirit

Kazan, like many other Russian cities, features a variety of festivals and other cultural events throughout the year, many of which are international and cosmopolitan in their scope. Music festivals devoted to opera and jazz roll through the city in February and August, respectively, while a high-profile festival dedicated to Muslim cinema from around the world returns every September.

Discover Local Tatar Culture
Of course, a trip to Kazan presents plenty of opportunities to experience and celebrate local Tatar Culture, whether that entails shopping for clothing items as above, sampling Tatar cuisine as below, or participating in the Karavon Festival in May, which takes places not only in Kazan but throughout the Republic. If you're interested in Tatar Culture, this might be the best time of year to visit Tatarstan!

...and Tasty Tatar Cuisine
Tatar food is a bit more evergreen than conspicuous displays of traditional culture, though some items seem more appropriate in warm or cold weather than others. *Ukha* fish soup, for example, is a more welcome choice to slurp down

during the frigid winter months, while *chak-chak* doughnuts are more palatable when the temperature rises into the 80s and 90s.

Ride a Riverboat (During the Summer)
Speaking of the warmer months, it is during this period exclusively (May to October, give or take) when boats travel on the Volga River that runs through Kazan. While some companies do exist for the purpose of taking tourists on pleasure rides along the river, you should keep in mind that many of these boats are essentially water buses. While this means they're affordable, they can also be quite crowded, making for an authentic experience, but a less than idyllic one.

Get Out of Town
Kazan is the capital of Tatarstan, but it's not all there is to the Republic. You could take a day trip to Raifa Monastery, which sits on the shores of a lake whose chilly waters are perfect for a dip

during the summer. The town of Bolgar is a little farther (if you do visit on a day trip, it'll be a very long day), but has been important throughout Russian history, and is currently a pilgrimage site for Muslims. Finally, Christopol feels more like the rest of Russia, with a 1700s aesthetic that may have you feel like you're in the time of Catherine the Great—or closer to Helsinki than to Istanbul, as it were.

Rub Shoulders with The Locals in Bauman Street
Bauman Street, the main pedestrian thoroughfare, pumps life through the city centre both day and night. Alongside souvenir shops sit cafés, shops and museums with street performers and buskers out to entertain. At night people who are out looking for a good time fill up the restaurants, clubs, and bars that the strip has to offer. One of the oldest streets in Kazan, even a casual stroll down it will take you past beautiful sights such as

the iconic bell tower for the Epiphany Church and the unique Monument Cat Kazan.

Get A Culture Hit at The Hermitage-Kazan Center
Lesser-known than its sibling museum in St. Petersburg, the Hermitage Kazan is still a must-visit for art lovers. Many exhibitions comprehensively showcase both Russian and international art across artistic periods and mediums. Housed in a former Junker school, the building's architecture dates back to the early 19th century and the elegant interiors are eye-catching works of art in themselves.

Explore The Kremlin
World Heritage-listed, the Kazan Kremlin is the only surviving Tatar fortress in Russia, parts of it dating back to the 16th and 17th centuries. Built at the request of the Ivan the Terrible, the bright white sandstone walls encircle the city's historical centre filled with age-old buildings. Highlights

include the Kul Sharif Mosque, the Hermitage and the Tatarstan Museum of Natural History.

Eat Tatar Food
Sample the flavours of Tatarstan at any of the outstanding restaurants and cafés that have earned Kazan its reputation as a haven for foodies. Influenced by both Russian and Eastern cuisine, soups, dairy and beets feature just as much as sesame seeds and savoury, Turkish style pastries. Those with a sweet tooth shouldn't miss the Museum of Chak-Chak, an interactive space dedicated to traditional tartar food and drinks, in particular *chak-chak* honey baked balls of dough, served at celebrations and festivities.

Be Inspired by The Temple of All Religions
As a multi-faith place of worship, the inclusivity of religious beliefs systems is a driving force in the Temple of All Religions' design. Created by local artist, architect and benefactor Ildar Khanov and a

team of assistants he met through his work in rehabilitation services, the delightful jumble of colours and design draws on sixteen different faiths for inspiration. Sixteen minarets, spires and cupolas are coloured with neon greens, yellows and azures, each embellished with with a Christian cross, the Star of David or Muslim crescent, representing the unification of the major religions under one roof.

4 Arakchinskoye Shosse, Poselok Staroye Arakchino Kazan, Respublika Tatarstan, 420079, Russia. +79870023995

Ponder Matters of the Heart at Syuyumbike Tower
The legend of the tower says that after Ivan the Terrible seized Kazan he then wanted to wed Princess Syuyumbike, who was less than impressed with the idea. She convinced Ivan that she would marry him on the condition he built a tower higher than any the city already had. He obliged and

under the guise of taking in the view, Syuyumbike went up to the top and flung herself off, so to avoid the impending marriage. While this fable has managed to linger throughout the years, it is estimated that construction of the 58-metre tower occurred in the 17th or 18th century, long after Ivan the Terrible, when tiered, wedding-cake like buildings were popular. Ulitsa Sheynkmana, Kazan, Respublika Tatarstan, 420111, Russia

Visit The Soviet Lifestyle Museum
Over-flowing with kitsch knick-knacks, trinkets and relics of a time now long gone, the quirky Soviet Lifestyle Museum pays homage to the cultural happenings during life under the Iron Curtain. Based in a former communal apartment, the collection spans from the 1930s to the 1990s. While most of the memorabilia relates to the music and art of that era, there is a Soviet secondary school experience exhibition as well as a

rack of vintage soviet clothes visitors can dress up in. Ulitsa Sheynkmana, Kazan, Respublika Tatarstan, 420111, Russia

Soak Up the Local Atmosphere at The Central Market

Echoing Tatar bazars of yore, Kazan's central market is a vibrant reminder of life in bygone times. Vendors push their wares and rub shoulders with *babushkas* selling produce straight from their garden, or berries and mushrooms foraged from nearby forests. An onslaught of smells, tastes and sights, the central market is the place to be to soak up local atmosphere, buy souvenirs, or get stuck into a tasty lunch.

The End

www.ingramcontent.com/pod-product-compliance
Lightning Source LLC
Chambersburg PA
CBHW031117080526
44587CB00011B/1011